VIOLIN

Disney's
Beauty
and the
Beast

Artwork © The Walt Disney Company

D1091490

Hal Leonard Publishing Corporation

7777 West Bluemound Road P.O. Box 13819 Milwaukee, WI 53213

BELLE

Violin

Lyrics by HOWARD ASHMAN
Music by ALAN MENKEN

4

CODA I

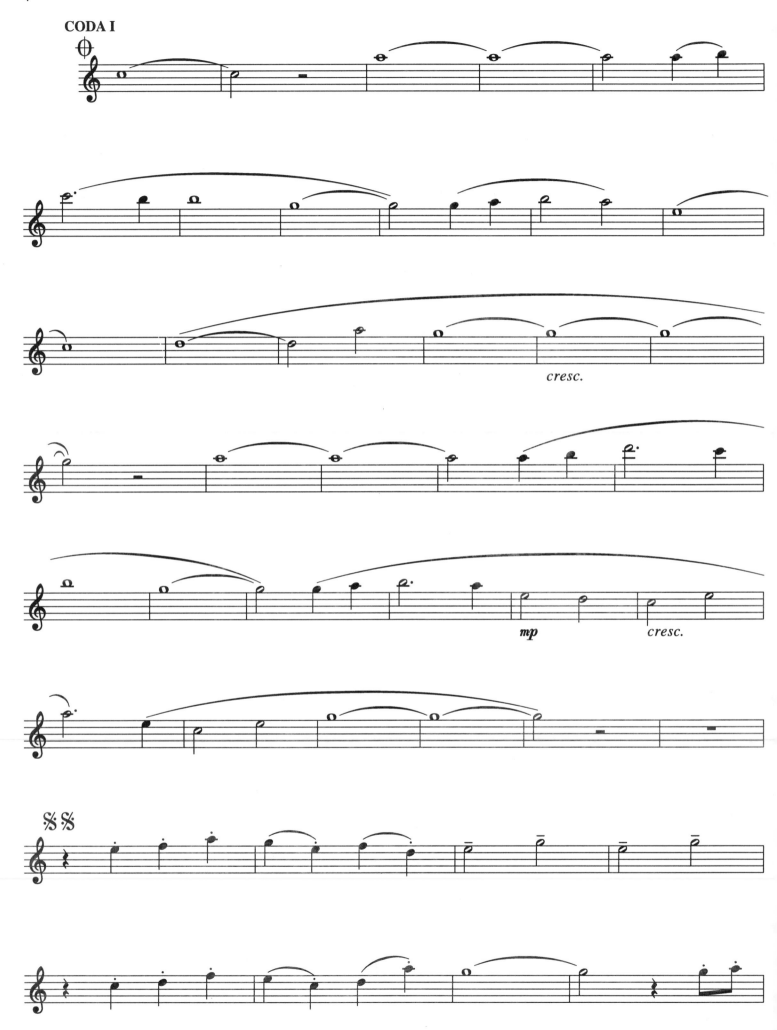

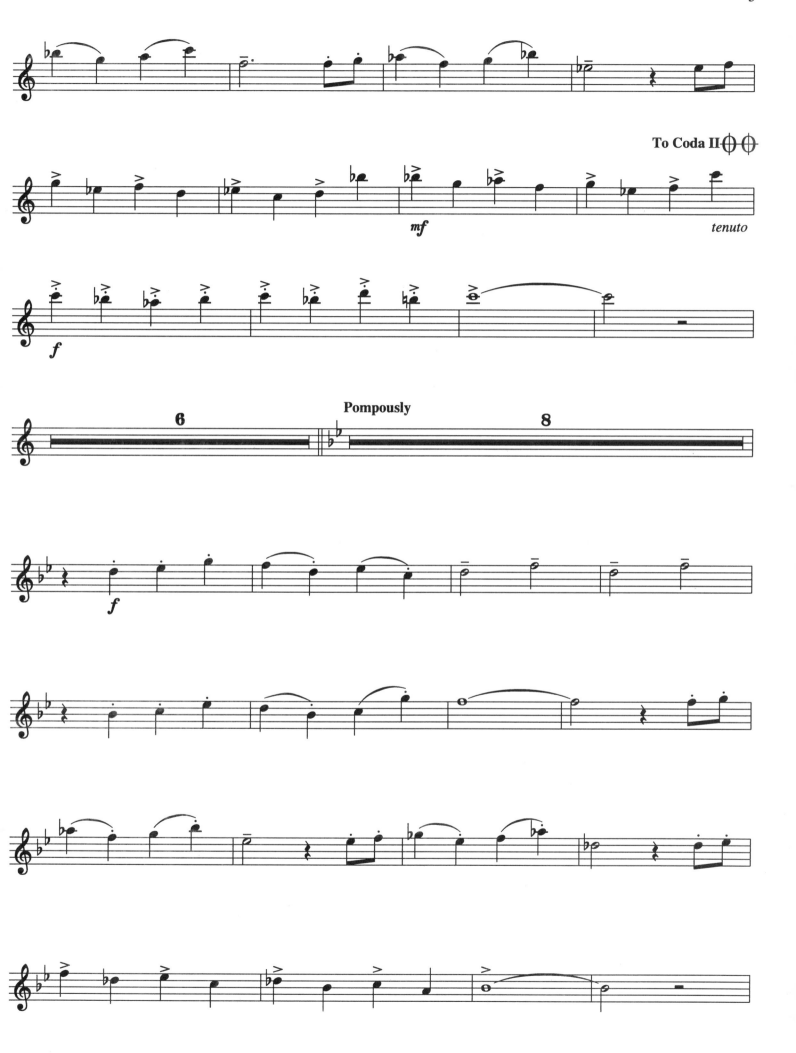

6

BELLE (REPRISE)

Lyrics by HOWARD ASHMAN
Music by ALAN MENKEN

Violin

GASTON

Lryics by HOWARD ASHMAN
Music by ALAN MENKEN

Violin

Bright Waltz

mf

f

cresc.   *rit.*

Barroom Waltz (played in one)

f

a tempo

GASTON (REPRISE)

Lyrics by HOWARD ASHMAN
Music by ALAN MENKEN

Violin

BE OUR GUEST

Violin

Lyrics by HOWARD ASHMAN
Music by ALAN MENKEN

Moderate tempo

13

SOMETHING THERE

Lyrics by HOWARD ASHMAN
Music by ALAN MENKEN

Violin

THE MOB SONG

Lyrics by HOWARD ASHMAN
Music by ALAN MENKEN

Violin

BEAUTY AND THE BEAST

Lyrics by HOWARD ASHMAN
Music by ALAN MENKEN

Violin

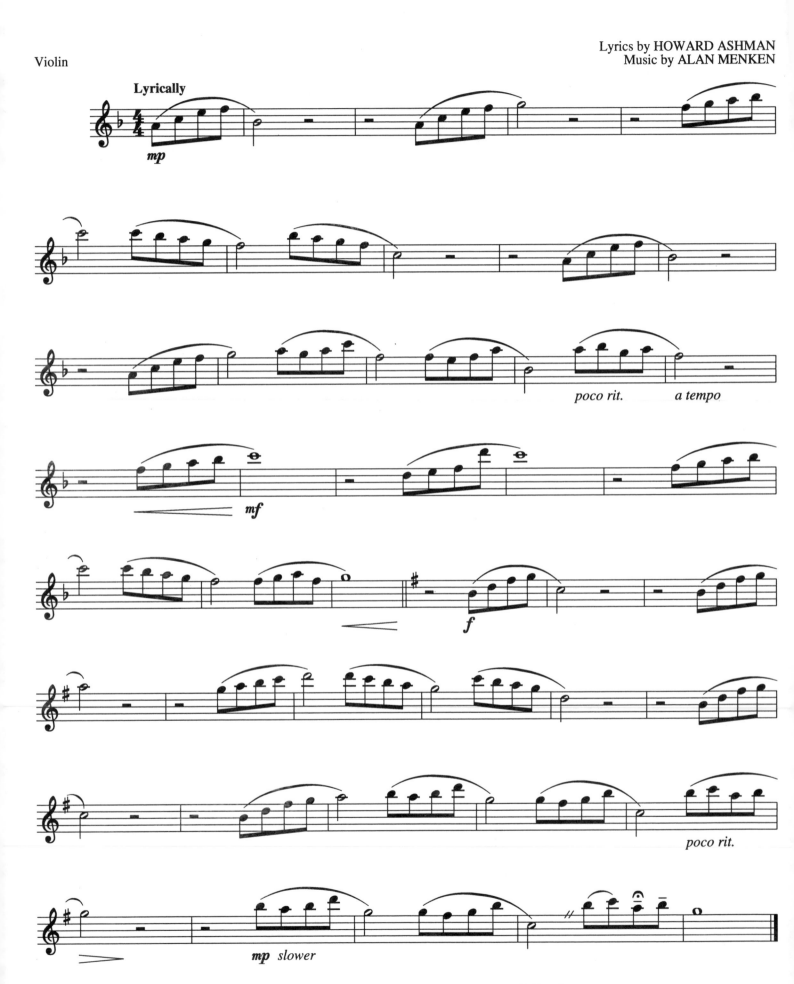